Center for Development *of* Security Excellence

Student
Handbook

Learn. Perform. Protect.

DEFENSE SECURITY SERVICE

Center for Development of Security Excellence | 938 Elkridge Landing Road, Linthicum, MD 21090

Return to Table of Contents

Welcome to the Center for Development of Security Excellence (CDSE). We encourage you to take advantage of all the training, education, and professionalization resources available to you through the CDSE.

Be assured that our program managers, instructors, educators, and support staff are committed to providing the security community with products and services that facilitate enhancement, development, and collaboration. Best wishes for your success in your professional growth.

Very respectfully,

Kevin J. Jones
Director, CDSE

Return to Table of Contents

TABLE OF CONTENTS

About Defense Security Service

Contributing To National Security

The Defense Security Service (DSS) is an agency of the Department of Defense (DoD) located in Quantico, Virginia with field offices throughout the United States. The Under Secretary of Defense for Intelligence provides authority, direction and control over DSS. DSS provides the military services, Defense agencies, 24 Federal agencies and approximately 13,300 cleared contractor facilities with security support services.

The Center for Development of Security Excellence (CDSE) is located in Linthicum, Md., and provides security education and training to security professionals through formal classroom and distributed learning methodologies (i.e., computer-based, web-based and tele-training).

DSS Mission

On behalf of the Department of Defense and other U.S. Government Departments and Agencies, the Defense Security Service supports national security and the warfighter through our security oversight and education missions. DSS oversees the protection of U.S. and foreign classified information and technologies in the hands of industry under the National Industrial Security Program (NISP) and serves as the functional manager for the DoD security professional development program. We provide security education, training, and professional development services as the functional manager for the DoD security professional development program, and for other U.S. Government personnel and contractor employees, and representatives of foreign governments, as required.

DSS Vision

Be the focal point of interaction and premier provider of industrial security and education services for the U.S. Government and the companies in the National Industrial Security Program in support of national security.

Return to Table of Contents

About CDSE

The Center for Development of Security Excellence (CDSE) Directorate is located in Linthicum, Md. , and oversees the missions of Security Education, Training, and Security Professionalization.

CDSE Mission

Provide the DoD with a security center of excellence for the professionalization of the security community and be the premier provider of security education and training for the DoD and industry under the National Industrial Security Program (NISP). The CDSE provides development, delivery, and exchange of security knowledge to ensure a high-performing workforce capable of addressing our Nation's security challenges.

CDSE Vision

To be the premier provider and center of excellence for security education, training, and professionalization for the DoD and industry under the NISP.

Return to Table of Contents

About Education Division

The CDSE Education Division offers courses designed specifically to develop leaders for the DoD security community. These courses are similar in scope to college and graduate level courses. Most courses are a semester long. Courses are delivered using a collaborative online learning environment, making them available to U.S. military members and government employees worldwide. Some courses also include opportunities for mid-career security professionals to study and learn together in a classroom setting for part of the semester. No tuition or fees are required to take CDSE courses; however, some courses require the purchase of textbooks. For additional information about the Education Division please click here: http://www.cdse.edu/education.

About Training Division

The CDSE Training Division embraces the training challenges facing the DoD security community and our industry partners in the 21st century. The Training Division offers over 150 diverse training courses and products presented through a variety of learning platforms. CDSE courses and products continuously meet the needs of our target population and are streamlined to the performance requirements and busy schedules of the contemporary learner. The CDSE also offers credit recommendations for certain courses through its affiliation with the American Council on Education's College Credit Recommendation Service (ACE CREDIT).

CDSE's award-winning training reflects the expertise of knowledgeable security training professionals dedicated to producing and delivering effective, engaging training and associated resources, presented using cutting edge technology-based instruction methods, virtual environments, and eLearning courseware.

Courses and products are available across functional areas and through various delivery platforms; instructor-led, eLearning, podcasts, shorts, videos, webinars, resources and job aids.

Disciplines

- Counterintelligence
- Cybersecurity
- General Security
- Industrial Security
- Information Security
- International Security
- Operations Security
- Personnel Security
- Physical Security
- Sensitive Compartmented Information
- Special Access Programs

About Professionalization Division

Workforce professionalization…the pathway to a successful and rewarding career in the DoD security environment. The Professionalization Division aligns security education, training, and certification products, services, activities, and initiatives providing a synchronized and systematic approach in providing career services that meet the needs of security practitioners, today and for the future. Oversight of the DoD Security Standards ensures that security practitioners receive the training, education, and professional development required to address the knowledge, tasks, and skills required to be able to perform.

CDSE products and services complement Component initiatives to professionalize the workforce. CDSE's Outreach and Communication efforts strengthen the bonds with the DoD Security Enterprise by participation in and at security-themed workshops, events and conferences and continued liaison across the communities.

About Office of the Registrar

The administration and integration of the services provided by the CDSE Education, Professionalization, and Training Divisions are accomplished through the support offered by the Office of the Registrar. This office has administrative oversight of the Security Training, Education and Professionalization Portal (STEPP). STEPP is the gateway for students to access training and education courses and to establish interest in the SPēD certification program. STEPP is also the system the Registrar utilizes to provide a variety of student support services to our DoD security professional students. Those services include, but are not limited to, the collection, management, and maintenance of accurate student profile information; student academic and enrollment records; assisting students with registration matters; transcript requests; verifying eligibility status related to scheduling courses and assessments; and a host of other services.

Return to Table of Contents

GENERAL INFORMATION

Directions to CDSE

The Center for Development of Security Excellence is located at 938 Elkridge Landing Road, Linthicum, MD 21090.

From Washington DC/ Northern VA:

- Take I-95 North to Route 295 North (Baltimore-Washington Parkway).
- Proceed approximately 20 miles.
- Take the W. Nursery Road exit.
- Bear right at the light at the end of the ramp onto W. Nursery Road. Remain in the right lane.
- Turn right at the third light onto Winterson Road.
- Turn left at the next light onto Elkridge Landing Road.
- Take the very next right into the parking areas. CDSE is ahead on the right. The number 938 is on the upper left front of the building.
- The Student Parking lot is immediately on the left after turning off of Elkridge Landing Road.

From Baltimore:

- Take I-95 South to I-695 East.
- Take I-695 East to Route 295 South (Baltimore-Washington Parkway).
- Take the W. Nursery Road exit.
- Turn left at the light at the end of the ramp onto W. Nursery Road.
- Turn right at the fourth light onto Winterson Road.
- Turn left at the next light onto Elkridge Landing Road.
- Take the very next right into the parking areas. CDSE is ahead on the right. The number 938 is on the upper left front of the building.
- The Student Parking lot is immediately on the left after turning off of Elkridge Landing Road.

From Baltimore Washington International (BWI) Thurgood Marshall Airport:

- CDSE is a 5 to 10 minute drive from BWI Airport.
- Follow Elm Road from the airport; turn right on Terminal Road; cross Rt. 170 (Airport Loop).
- Turn left at the light onto Elkridge Landing Road.
- Turn left off Elkridge Landing Road into the parking areas just before the light at Winterson Road. (This left is just past the SpringHill Suites by Marriott Hotel on the right.)
- CDSE is ahead on the right. The number 938 is on the upper left front of the building.

From the BWI Car Rental Facility (located at 7432 New Ridge Road, Hanover, MD 21076)

- Drive northeast on New Ridge Road from the facility.
- Turn right onto Stoney Run Road.
- Take the 1st right and remain right onto Route 170 North / Aviation Blvd.
- Go about 1.7 miles and turn left at the light for Terminal Road.
- Immediately turn left at the next light at Elkridge Landing Road.
- Go about 1.7 miles and turn left off Elkridge Landing Road into the parking areas just before the light at Winterson Road.
(This left is just past the SpringHill Suites by Marriott Hotel on the right.)
- CDSE is ahead on the right. The number 938 is on the upper left front of the building.

Please refer to the Student Parking Map on page 10

Return to Table of Contents

Parking

Please park in the designated area. CDSE shares the parking lots with tenants of other buildings and parking in an inappropriate area can result in your vehicle being towed. Please refer to the Parking Map on next page.

CDSE Student Parking Lot

- After turning into the parking areas off Elkridge Landing Road, the designated Student Parking Lot is located immediately on the right. Student Parking signs are posted at the entrance.
- To enter the CDSE, exit the CDSE Student Parking entrance to the right and walk to the building on the right. Number 938 is on the upper left front of the building. Enter through the front door.

Overflow Parking Lot *(also for students)*

- From Elkridge Landing Road, turn left onto Winterson Road and continue past the first parking lot entrance by the CDSE building
- Turn left into the Candlewood Suites entrance.
- Follow the signs to FANX Overflow Parking and park.
- Walk from the Overflow Lot to the sidewalk heading back to the buildings closest to Winterson Road. CDSE is the first building at the end of this sidewalk. Enter through the front door.
  - or –
- Walk on Winterson Road from the Candlewood Suites entrance to the first building on the right. Enter through the front door.

Please refer to the Student Parking Map on page 10. Student parking is shaded green.

Return to Table of Contents

CDSE Parking Map
938 Elkridge Landing Road | Linthicum, MD 21090

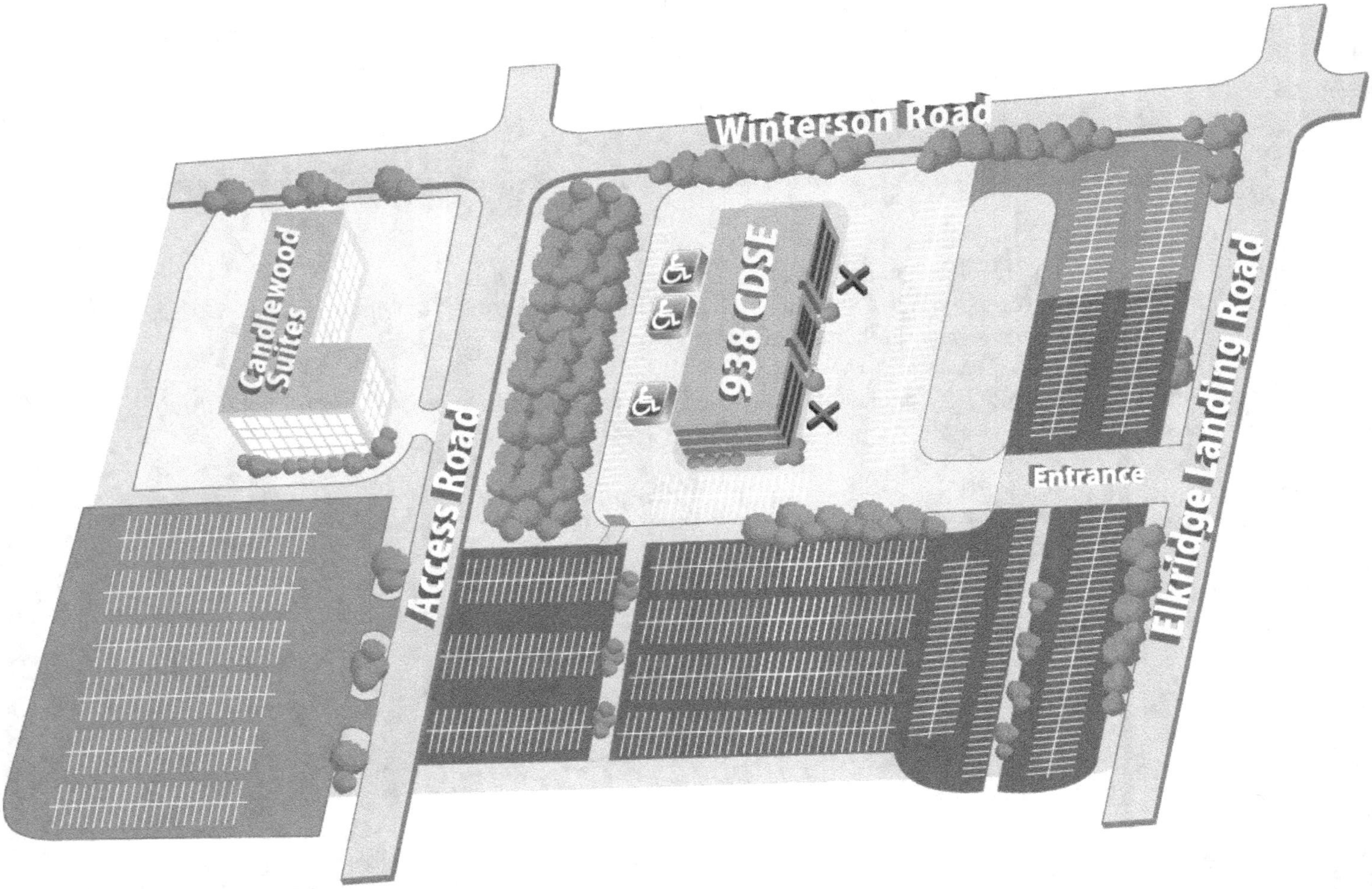

Winterson Road

Candlewood Suites

938 CDSE

Access Road

Entrance

Elkridge Landing Road

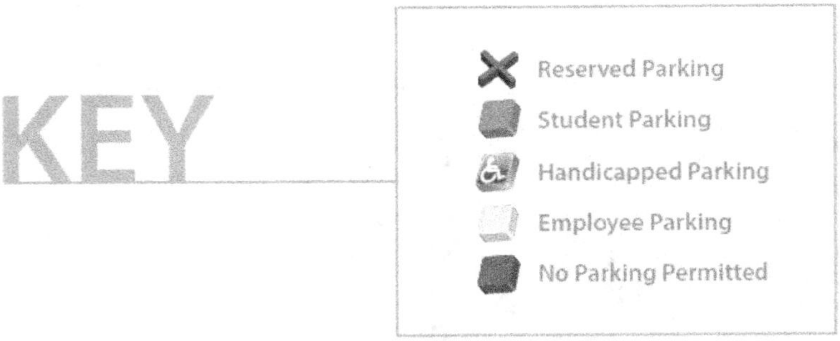

KEY

 Reserved Parking

 Student Parking

 Handicapped Parking

 Employee Parking

 No Parking Permitted

Return to Table of Contents

Building Hours

Students can enter the building at any time between 0730 and 1700. Please enter from the front of the building and have a photo ID in hand for check-in on the first day of class. Classes end at approximately 1700.

Special Needs

The CDSE supports the Americans with Disabilities Act of 1990. Students, visiting instructors, and other CDSE guests with special needs should contact the CDSE Registrar at least two weeks prior to arrival by sending an email to CDSE.Registrar.Support@dss.mil.

Arrival/In-Processing

Photo identification (i.e., driver's license or passport) is required for entry to the facility. Please arrive 15 to 30 minutes early to check in at the front desk.

Dress Code

The CDSE standard for dress and appearance is business casual. Khaki slacks and polo shirts are acceptable; apparel such as tank tops, sorts, sweat suits, tennis shoes, or jeans are not acceptable. Civilian attire is preferred for military personnel. Please remember to bring a jacket as our heating and cooling system is temperamental.

ID Badges

Badges for students are issued at the reception desk or in the classroom, and badges for guests and visitors are issued at the reception desk.

Visits from foreign nationals must be coordinated through the CDSE Security Coordinator at (410) 865-3245.

Attendance

Students are expected to attend all scheduled sessions on time. Contact the course manager as soon as possible regarding absences from class. Absences may result in a course incompletion or failure.

Internet Access

Computers are available in the Student Resource Center. Password information is located at the computer stations. Please note that WiFi is not available in the building.

CDSE Telephone/Fax

CDSE Front Desk:
(410) 865-3113/3114
Fax machines:
(410) 865-3139 – Front Desk
(410) 865-3182 – CDSE
(410) 865-2719 – Registrar's Office

Return to Table of Contents

Smoking Areas

The only designated smoking area for the building is the outside break area with the picnic tables (on the Winterson Road end of the building).

Lost and Found

The reception desk in the CDSE lobby, serves as the Lost and Found for the CDSE. Please contact the receptionist at (410) 865-3113/3114 if something is lost or found.

Medical Problems/Emergencies

There are several first aid kits located throughout the CDSE building. A defibrillator is located at the Front Desk in the lobby. Students will fill out an emergency contact form in the classroom.

Inclement Weather/Emergency Closures

In the event of inclement weather, or any other event that might require early dismissal from or closing of the CDSE building in Linthicum, MD, students should call (410) 865-3232 for up-to-date information.

Comments/Concerns/Complaints

The CDSE wants students to be successful and enjoy their learning experiences. While attending any CDSE course, students are encouraged to share comments, concerns, complaints, or grievances directly with the course instructor. Should the concern involve an instructor, students should contact the CDSE at DSS.CDSE@dss.mil.

If that process is pursued without satisfaction, students may write or call the Commission of the Council on Occupational Education, 7840 Roswell Rd., Building 300, Suite 325, Atlanta, GA 30350, or call (770) 396-3898 or (800) 917-2081.

CDSE Food Facilities

The first floor Cantina / Break Room offers ample seating, several microwaves, a refrigerator, vending machines with sodas, hot beverages, and snacks, a television, and several telephones.

Return to Table of Contents

Return to Table of Contents

HOTELS

1. **Candlewood Suites Baltimore-Extended Stay**
   1247 Winterson Road, Linthicum, MD
   (410) 850-9214

2. **Comfort Suites BWI Airport Linthicum Heights**
   815 Elkridge Landing Road, Linthicum, MD
   (410) 691-1000

3. **Courtyard Baltimore BWI Airport**
   1671 West Nursery Road, Linthicum, MD
   (410) 859-8855

4. **Embassy Suites Hotel Baltimore-BWI Airport**
   1300 Concourse Drive, Linthicum, MD
   (410) 850-0747

5. **La Quinta Inn-Airport**
   1734 W Nursery Road, Linthicum, MD
   (410) 859-2333

6. **Hampton Inn BWI Airport**
   829 Elkridge Landing Road, Linthicum, MD
   (443) 203-5156

7. **Hilton Baltimore BWI Airport**
   1739 West Nursery Road, Linthicum, MD
   (410) 694-0808

8. **Doubletree by Hilton Baltimore BWI Airport Hotel**
   890 Elkridge Landing Road, Linthicum, MD
   (410) 859-8400

9. **Homewood Suites by Hilton**
   1181 Winterson Road, Linthicum, MD
   (410) 684-6100

10. **Hyatt Place Baltimore BWI Airport**
    940 International Drive, Linthicum Heights, MD 21090
    (410) 859-3366

11. **Marriott - BWI Airport**
    1743 West Nursery Road, Linthicum Heights, MD
    (410) 859-8300

12. **Microtel Inn and Suites - Baltimore Maryland**
    1170 Winterson Road, Linthicum, MD
    (410) 865-7500

13. **Red Roof Inn**
    827 Elkridge Landing Road, Linthicum, MD
    (410) 850-7600

14. **Residence Inn Baltimore BWI Airport**
    1160 Winterson Road, Linthicum, MD
    (410) 691-0255

15. **Sheraton BWI Hotel**
    1100 Old Elkridge Landing Road, Linthicum, MD
    (443) 577-2100

16. **SpringHill Suites Baltimore BWI Airport**
    899 Elkridge Landing Road, Linthicum, MD
    (410) 694-0555

17. **Staybridge Suites BWI Extended Stay Hotel**
    1301 Winterson Road, Linthicum, MD
    (410) 850-5666

18. **TownePlace Suites Baltimore BWI Airport**
    1171 Winterson Road, Linthicum, MD
    (410) 694-0060

19. **Westin BWI Airport**
    1110 Old Elkridge Landing Road, Linthicum, MD 21090
    (443) 577-2310

Refer to map on the next page for locations.

Return to Table of Contents

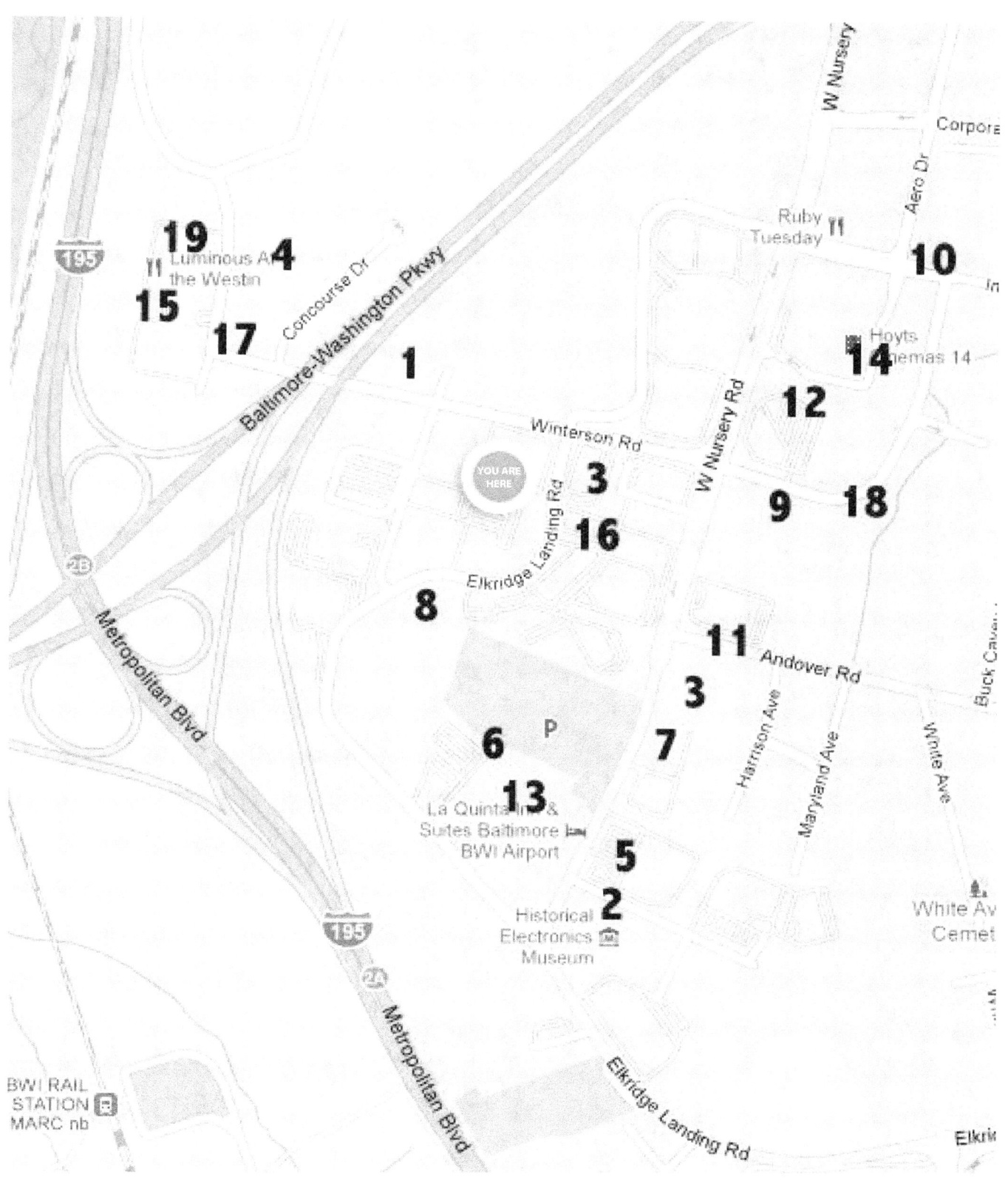

Return to Table of Contents

RESTAURANTS

1. **Gateway Deli**
   1302 Concourse Drive, Linthicum, MD
   (410) 850-5084

2. **Adamm's Airport Deli**
   891 Elkridge Landing Road, Linthicum, MD
   (410) 850-4333

3. **Ruby Tuesday's**
   950 International Drive, Linthicum, MD
   (410) 694-0031

4. **Bob Evans**
   996 Corporate Boulevard, Linthicum, MD
   (410) 684-2102

5. **Wendy's**
   1589 W. Nursery Road, Linthicum, MD
   (410) 850-0694

6. **Starbucks**
   1700 W. Nursery Road, Linthicum, MD
   (410) 859-1233

7. **Quiznos**
   823 Elkridge Landing Road, Linthicum, MD
   (410) 850-4430

8. **McDonald's**
   778A Elkridge Landing Road, Linthicum, MD
   (410) 859-8983

9. **Domino's Pizza**
   506 S. Camp Meade Road, Linthicum, MD
   (410) 684-3030

10. **Subway**
    529 S. Camp Meade Road, Linthicum, MD
    (410) 859-2445

11. **Papa John's Pizza**
    529 S. Camp Meade Road, Linthicum, MD
    (410) 684-2777

12. **Ocean (Chinese)**
    529 Camp Meade Road, Linthicum, MD
    (410) 691-2222

13. **Matsu (Japanese)**
    517 S. Camp Meade Road, Linthicum, MD
    (410) 850-0009

14. **Squisito too (Italian)**
    419 S. Camp Meade Road, Linthicum, MD
    (410) 684-6868

15. **KFC**
    708 W. Nursery Road, Linthicum, MD
    (410) 789-1727

16. **Taco Bell**
    5184 Raynor Avenue, Linthicum, MD
    (410) 789-5085

17. **Season's Pizza**
    810 Nursery Road, Linthicum, MD
    (410) 609-1002

18. **G&M Restaurant & Carryout**
    804 Hammonds Ferry Road, Linthicum, MD
    (410) 636-1777

19. **Olive Grove**
    705 N. Hammonds Ferry Road, Linthicum, MD
    (410) 636-1385

20. **700 South Gourmet Deli & Cafe**
    1190 Winterson Road, Linthicum, MD
    (410) 859-1701

Refer to the map on next page for locations.

Return to Table of Contents

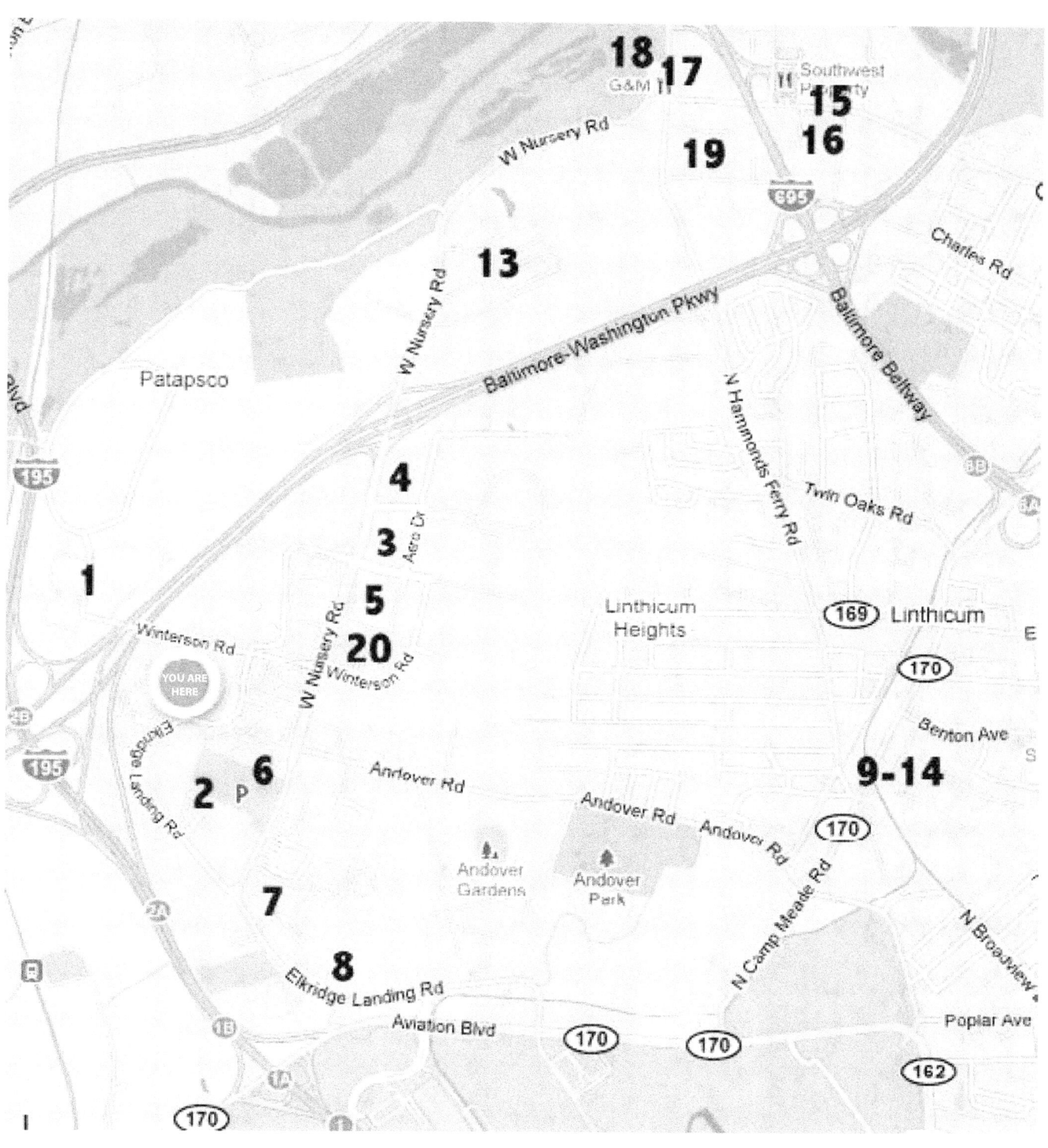

Return to Table of Contents

Banking

Wells Fargo
721 N. Hammonds Ferry Road
Linthicum, MD
(410) 609-0368

Bank of America
201 Benton Avenue #1
Linthicum, MD
(410) 859-0200

M&T Bank
801 Elkridge Landing Road
Linthicum, MD
(410) 850-4051

Healthcare/ Hospital/Urgent Care

Baltimore/Washington Medical Center
301 Hospital Drive
Glen Burnie, MD
(410) 787-4000

Guardian Protection Services
510 McCormick Dr.
Glen Burnie, MD
(410)760-4836

Patient First
7116 Ritchie Hwy.
Glen Burnie, MD
(443)577-0277

Pharmacies

CVS Pharmacy
7095 Baltimore Annapolis Blvd.
Glenn Burnie, MD
(410)859-3113

Rite Aid
7270 Montgomery Rd.
Elkridge, MD
(410) 796-3344

Dentist

Michael J. Daciek, DDS
411 S. Camp Meade Road
Linthicum, MD
(410) 850-0505

Post Office

U.S. Post Office
515 S. Camp Meade Road
Linthicum, MD
(410) 859-9886

Laundry and Dry Cleaning

Linthicum Laundromat
521 S. Camp Meade Road
Linthicum, MD
(410) 859-0310

Movie Theater

Hoyts West Nursery Cinema
1591 West Nursery Road
Linthicum, MD
(410) 850-8999

Return to Table of Contents

Local Attractions

Baltimore Inner Harbor (approximately 16 minutes from CDSE)

Baltimore's Inner Harbor is one of the most photographed and visited areas of the city. It has been one of the major seaports in the United States since the 1700s and started blossoming into the cultural center of Baltimore in the 1970s.

Distinct in function and form, locals and visitors enjoy the Inner Harbor and its surrounding neighborhoods that offer a variety of fine dining, cultural experiences, and exciting nightlife.

From breath-taking panoramic views of the skyline from the Observation Level of the World Trade Center to the up-close and personal experiences of street performances happening spontaneously at the waterfront, Baltimore's Inner Harbor offers a variety of things to see and do.

Inner Harbor Restaurants

Elegant gourmet cuisine and ethnic foods from around the world and plenty of fresh seafood from Maryland's Chesapeake Bay abound. Sample a taste of Baltimore at one of the many Inner Harbor restaurants.

Harborplace and the Gallery

200 E. Pratt Street
Baltimore, MD
Phone: (410) 332-4191

Located in the heart of the Inner Harbor on Pratt Street, Harborplace and the Gallery offer unique shopping, diverse dining, and a variety of entertainment right on the picturesque waterfront.

Spirit Cruises - Baltimore

561 Light Street
Baltimore, MD
Phone: (866) 312-2469

The newly renovated Spirit of Baltimore offers year-round lunch and dinner cruises as well as specialty and holiday cruises. The Spirit has two fully enclosed climate-controlled decks along with an open air panoramic deck that boasts the best views of the historic Harbor. The Inner Harbor Spirit offers interactive, narrated 60-minute sightseeing tours of Baltimore from April through October.

Maryland Science Center

601 Light Street
Baltimore, MD
Phone: (410) 545-5927

Let your senses and your mind wander as you experience the numerous sights and hands-on activities at the Maryland Science Center. It features an IMAX theater and a planetarium that's sure to please everyone.

Baltimore Aquarium

501 E. Pratt Street, Pier 3
Baltimore, MD
Phone: (410) 576-3800

The National Aquarium in Baltimore houses sharks, dolphins, rays, and tropical fish among the more than 16,000 creatures in naturalistic exhibits, including a walk-through rain forest, an exciting live-action dolphin show, and a new Australian exhibit.

Return to Table of Contents

World Trade Center

401 E. Pratt Street
Baltimore, MD
Phone: (410) 837-8439

Seeming to hover 405 feet directly over top of the harbor, the World Trade Center in Baltimore offers the best view of the city in every direction from the "Top of the World" Observation Level on the 27th floor. Constructed in 1977, its 32 floors make up the world's tallest equilateral 5-sided building.

Fort McHenry

2400 E. Fort Avenue
Baltimore, MD
Phone: (410) 962-4290

A water-taxi ride away, you can learn about the Battle of Baltimore and the nation's history by visiting Fort McHenry. Fireworks conclude Flag Day and Defender's Day celebrations. Special events include living history weekends where the Fort McHenry Guard performs demonstrations.

Ed Kane's Water Taxi

1735 Lancaster Street
Baltimore, MD
Phone: (410) 563-3901

For the perfect transportation in and around Baltimore's Inner Harbor, the water taxi is an affordable solution. Located on Lancaster Street, one price buys unlimited rides for the day, and group discount rates are available. Native Baltimore residents and frequent city visitors often opt for the frequent floater annual pass.

Historic Ships in Baltimore

Pier 1; 301 E. Pratt Street
Baltimore, MD 21202
Phone: (410) 539-1797

From fighting the Transatlantic slave trade to daring rescues on the Chesapeake; from riding out hurricanes to proving humanitarian aid and defending the freedons we hold dear, Historic Ships in Baltimore provides "hands-on encounters with history." Tours and activities, live cannon firings, educational programs, and more.

Baltimore Orioles

333 W. Camden Street
Oriole Park at Camden Yards
Baltimore, MD
Phone: (888) 848-BIRD

A visit to Camden Yards is just minutes away and, if you're a true baseball fan, be sure to see the Baltimore Orioles Hall of Fame exhibit and the Babe Ruth Birthplace and Museum located nearby. You can also visit the Sports Legends Museum, which offers 22,000 square feet of artifacts and interactive exhibits, transforming Camden Station into one of the most spectacular sports museums in America.

Return to Table of Contents

Baltimore Ravens

1101 Russell Street
M&T Bank Stadium
Baltimore, MD
Phone: (410) 261-7283

Get in on the spirit of the Purple and Black when you attend a Baltimore Ravens football game at the M&T Bank Stadium just a short distance from the Inner Harbor.

Port Discovery Children's Museum

35 Market Place
Baltimore, MD
Phone: (410) 727-8120

Discovery Children's Museum provides experiences that ignite imagination, inspire learning, and nurture growth through play. The Museum offers three floors of educational, interactive and hands-on/minds-on experiences designed for children ages 2 through 10.

Baltimore & Ohio Railroad Museum

901 W. Pratt Street
Baltimore, MD
Phone: (410) 752-2490

Where America's most important, historic, and comprehensive collection lives to tell the story of railroading every day. Forty acres of heritage and a world-class collection await your discovery!

Power Plant Live!

34 Market Place
Baltimore, MD
Phone: (410) 727-LIVE(5483)

A block away from Baltimore's Inner Harbor is Power Plant Live!, a premier dining and entertainment district featuring a variety of restaurants and nightclubs that surround a common plaza. There is also outdoor seating that often features live performances.

Baltimore Museum of Industry

1415 Key Highway
Baltimore, MD
Phone: (410) 727-4808

Visit re-created workshops, explore industry from days past, and see the 1906 Steam Tug Baltimore, a national historic landmark. Enjoy hands-on activities for kids, tours for the whole family, and free parking.

Return to Table of Contents

Important Links

Center for Development of Security Excellence: http://www.cdse.edu

Defense Security Service: http://www.dss.mil

STEPP username/password issues: http://www.dss.mil/about_dss/contact_dss/contact_dss.html

Important E-mail Addresses

Counterintelligence: Counterintelligence.training@dss.mil

Education Division: Education.cdse@dss.mil

General CDSE questions or concerns: CDSE@dss.mil

General Security questions: Generalsecurity.training@dss.mil

General Training questions: Training.CDSE@dss.mil

Industrial Security questions: Industrialsecurity.training@dss.mil

Information Security questions: Informationsecurity.training@dss.mil

Cybersecurity questions: Cybersecurity.training@dss.mil

JPAS training questions: JPAS.training@dss.mil

Physical Security questions: Physicalsecurity.training@dss.mil

Personnel Security questions: Personnelsecurity.training@dss.mil

Registrar/registration issues: CDSE.registrar.support@dss.mil

Sensitive Compartment Information questions: SCIsecurity.training@dss.mil

Special Access Program Security questions: SAPsecurity.training@dss.mil

Certification questions: SPeDCert@dss.mil

Important Phone Numbers

Front Desk: (410) 865-3113/3114

Inclement Weather /Emergency Closure Line: (410) 865-3232

Return to Table of Contents

Return to Table of Contents

www.ingramcontent.com/pod-product-compliance
Lightning Source LLC
Chambersburg PA
CBHW080405290526
45790CB00009BA/3714